It's What I've Got Left

Poems by Lisa Allen

LILY POETRY REVIEW BOOKS

Copyright © 2026 by Lisa Allen
Published by Lily Poetry Review Books
223 Winter Street
Whitman, MA 02382

https://lilypoetryreview.blog/

ISBN: 978-1-957755-70-0

All rights reserved. Published in the United States by Lily Poetry Review Books.
Library of Congress Control Number: 2026931725

The bottom line is I'm writing to save the dead. I'm writing to save the people I have lost, some of whose bodies are still walking around.

~Dorothy Allison

For A, N, & A/E
Always for A, N, & A/E

Table of Contents

1	Dear Reader	
2	Inheritance: A Broken Bop	
3	In the Down of the House of the Man on the Stoop	
4	Party Line	
5	Good Catholic Girls	
6	My Great Aunt Tells My Mother I Am Such a Good Girl	
8	No Need to Overthink	
9	On Maple Street	
10	Still Life With Recipe Card	
11	Every Star In the Sky	
12	Mina	
14	On Marjorie Drive	
15	It's Not Like She Didn't Teach Me Anything	
17	Bragging Rights	
18	In Prison, She	
19	The Sum of Me	
20	It's What I've Got Left	
21	The Sum of Me: Two	
22	Self-Portrait as Good Girl	
23	This Time When We Talk Things Are Different	
25	This Wind, Bitter	
27	A Proper Lady Speaks Not of Regret	
29	I Don't Pray Anymore But I Remember the Words	
31	Grandma, You're 97 Today	
32	The Quilt You Made Hangs In My Dining Room	
33	Who Loved You, Mina?	
35	Teaching Myself at 51	
36	Prolapse: Etymology	
37	Something That Made My Mother Sad	

40	You Turned 69 This April
41	When Grandma Visits at 4 A.M., She Does So As a Stinkbug
42	Mina Speaks
43	Twitter Says: Write Poems When You're Young
44	You, Too, Were a Novena
46	She Called Everyone Sweetheart
48	Lullaby
49	For All the People Who Say "But She's Your Mother! There Must Have Been Good Things Too."
50	I Think of You, Mom, As I Sit In the Driver's Seat of a U-Haul In a Fairfield Inn Parking Lot in Granite City, Illinois, Just This Past March
51	What Stories Would You Have Told Me If I'd Stayed?
52	My Therapist Says Joy is the Highest Form of Vulnerability
53	COVID Fever Dream of My Estranged Mother
54	A Dependent Clause
55	Grandma, I Didn't Get to Tell You
56	Dear Third Born Child, I Promise I'm Trying. Love, Mom.
57	Notes for My Daughter As She Plans Her Most Public Assault
61	Protecting the Nest
62	Mary, Do You See My Child In All Their Heavenly Splendor?
64	(Still) Want/ed To
66	Blue Mist
67	Smirk
68	Alternate Reality In Which I Return Home After Caring for My Mother
70	Notes
69	Acknowledgements
71	Gratitude

Dear Reader

we work to get over

and hide from each other

        bitter (shared) histories.

Name this illusion
        We are machines

caught in spin cycle, no end:

Before teeming mountains of laundry

        dwindle to spinster socks, before

the last smear of youth

        catches on crackled skin,

before eye meets eye

        in this toothpaste-speckled mirror:

remember our grandmothers and mothers

        and daughters

    one dies and another

carries the load:

We do. We don't. World without end.

Inheritance: A Broken Bop

I'll never shake you. Your words
lodged deep within—our history
helixed in every cell. I can
close my eyes, become young again
& hear the flick of your almost-empty Bic,
smell the exhale of your Marlboro Red.

I don't know the sound
of your voice anymore.

Do you know: fetal cells can breach
the placenta & lodge in a mother's brain,
stay until she dies—

Science tells me why, despite all these years gone, we hold on:
your grandmother's shame as she carried your mother &
your mother's bitterness as she carried you—our inheritance
spooling forward & back. Which traces of me are still
with you. These problems bewilder & fascinate: how
there was a you & me before there was a you, a me.

Which traces of me are still with you
when I don't know the sound
of your voice anymore.

Damn you science. I want to know why
you won't let me go, no matter how hard I try to stay
gone? Someday I'll ask my children which memories
of me won't let them go, try to trace them
to something we can name. I'll explain how we
carry both past & future, despite our own twisted ankles.

In the Down of the House of the Man on the Stoop

I am five, maybe eight. Spend my days at Grandma's house, the house that is her daughter's house, the house her daughter lived in with her husband and kids, my cousins—the house filled with CoolWhip containers and unsure mountains of fat-quarter fabric squares. I am five, maybe ten, the oldest of the cousins. Grandma's house is on one of the numbered streets—8th or 13th or maybe 6th. Grandma gives me money and sends me for milk, flour. Baking day: spitzbuben and bierocks, green bean dumpling soup. Cinnamon rolls. She wears a dirty apron, her cigarette smolders. The Young and the Restless whines from the living room. The screen door slams behind me, I turn right at the Miller's. Charlotte is my friend; we go for Suicides and cheesecakes after school, listen to Barbara Streisand and the Bee Gees. She is one of six, maybe ten, all girls except Scott. I think Scott is cute, wonder if thinking someone is cute is what it means to have a crush. I am five, maybe nine. I stop at each intersection: Cedar Street, Pine Street, Oak Street— look both ways before crossing. The man is there, sitting in the sun on his stoop on Fort Street, the only street that isn't a tree street. Whittling. I know that word—whittling—because the last time, the man told me it's another thing he does with his knife, said *it's how I shape my wood*. I know this word—whittling—because it's the only word that makes the man on the stoop smile, the only word of all his words that shows me his yellow teeth. I am five, maybe more, the steps of the stoop number that many. I count them as we go. The steps at Grandma's house go up. The steps at Charlotte's house go up. The steps of the man's house go down. Is that where I lose the money Grandma gave me? Is that where I—

Party Line

In the first house I remember, my father forced me to eat
fried bologna smothered in tomato sauce until I threw up.

Melamine plate—white rimmed
with blue roses, bluer leaves—

acid blooming
in my mouth.

His yelling, the lift
of his belt.

Ruffled yellow curtains, the rotary wall-mounted phone—wallpaper, maybe?

But I loved the kink of the phone cord, twirled
the rubbery coil around my fingers like princess curls. We dialed four numbers
to reach anyone else in town & sometimes caught strangers' conversations
cupped between our ears.

Party line, they called it.
It's called respect, he said.

Good Catholic Girls

don't talk like that don't
talk back don't
need to think
so hard it hurts

don't sleep naked do you
sleep naked maybe
call me when your kids leave
for school I'll teach you

how to stop my hurting how
to be my special girl let me
explain the word secret let me
show you what to do

kiddo, good girls like it
sometimes so much they beg
for more, good girls smile
when they swallow

what they want to say—kiddo
I'll forgive you if you
kneel, if you show me
how sorry you can be.

My Great Aunt Tells My Mother I Am Such a Good Girl

I remember the butterfly
brittle & pinned to the black
velvet of a shadow box.
How it hung next to her dresser.

She loved that butterfly,
the orange & yellow of its wings a riot
in that house of neutrals: the worn brown couch,
the black prayer books. Her wooden rosaries.
The unusual extravagance

pinioned. She & her sister,
the two who never married, alone
together in that cluttered house—

I pushed a chair to the dresser
& took that box from the wall. How delicate
those wings. How easily the first rip came—

an accident from my small hands.
But not the second. Or the eighth.
& I didn't stop

until all that was left intact was
the thorax. The abdomen, the proboscis.
The antenna. I didn't stop
until those wings were orange & yellow
confetti littering the bottom

of that black velvet box, didn't stop
until she took her frame, her gnarled fingers
soft on my five-year-old hands,
& stashed it in her closet. I didn't stop

until she filled that empty space
with a crucifix
borrowed from the living room wall.

No Need to Overthink

I misremember, he says. Mary Jane from down the block never
babysat so he and mom could see Elton John and Grandma Irene
died when I was in 8th grade, not 6th. But my brain knows—
someone I loved died every two years & I spent all of 13
waiting to see who was next, the same way a baker prays
over dough that refuses to rise, the proofing basket tattooing
rings on its polite underbelly. That summer, yet another *he*
watched me sink a foot into Wilson Lake, slapped
a mosquito that fed from the smooth of my ample ass.

On Maple Street

Let your mother tuck you in & turn out the light.
Watch her close the door. Practice
being quiet. Count spots on the ceiling.
Remember: don't blink.

It's safe when Rod Stewart spins
on the other side of your wall,
when cigarette smoke slides under the door.

Tiptoe from bed. Dress for school tomorrow:
pants and shirt, socks and shoes.
Brush your hair. Make the bed, except for
the top blanket.

Lay down. Cover up. Pretend it's a coffin.
Pray but don't move your lips.

Don't blink. When the light flames
above you close your eyes fast, so fast.
Maybe she didn't see. Pretend
you're a Chrissy doll, the one
you had to give your sister.

Stay so still when she pulls back
the pilly blue blanket. Wait for her to point
and cackle. Wait as she tells her friends,
now crowded in your room, to go back to their
dance. Don't wait for her to realize
you've started to cry.

Get up, like she says. Put on
your nightgown as she watches. Wait
until she closes the door,
until her friends sing again.

Still Life with Recipe Card

Cigarette smoke haze, kids running
room to room. Stacks of fat quarters

in every corner & boxes of Little Debbies
atop the fridge. December air

through the screen door. Victor & Nikki
on TV. Mountain Dew, iced tea, coffee. Cream.

Women childrearing. Women cleaning. Women
cooking, cleaning, bacon-bringing. Men drinking.

Men leaving. Casey Casum counting down.
Our buttered fingers dunked in sugar, licked clean.

Ringing phone, coiled cord. Our Father
& Glory Be. *Ach Jesùs guten himmel*, full-throated.

Her hands smoothing her apron, her hands
holding mine, her hands bent with age, folded light.

Every Star In the Sky

You let me walk by myself
from your house to Grandma's—
four blocks, maybe. Five.

You & she stood
on your porches, receivers
pressed against your faces,

hanging up only when Grandma
sees me. You both told me
this story over & over—

how big a girl I was, how you
could trust me to not stray.
But that couldn't be true,

could it? Your landline was mounted
on the kitchen wall & the kitchen
was at the back of your house.

Here's what's true: Sonny & Cher
was my favorite show & you let me
walk alone to watch it.

I was never out of sight.
The two of you, every star in the sky:
Your words still live

in my head: *trusted…not stray.*
The two of you, ends of an axis,
Then and now my north, my south.

Mina

As if allure to the past
could bring you back

with the right detail, like your smile
when you let me wiggle the fat

of your upper arm as you
held it up—I pretended it was

a swing & it was my job to push.
Or how you scolded me one night

in the bathtub, for letting the washcloth
linger too long on my five-year-old chest.

Or how you built a bed for me of chairs,
the backs turned rails to keep me from falling.

I still have the prayer book you made
and the tiny quilt. And your rosary.

I remember how fast you flew
through Hail Mary's and Glory Be's.

How you bragged to your neighbors
about the straight line I left

when I vacuumed your living room floor.
I don't remember a single meal

at the formica table in your kitchen
but I do recall the coconut

macaroons from Dillons that you hid
in the oven with the chocolate marshmallow

pinwheels you bought for Dad. Those
are $6 a package now. I stood in the cookie aisle

thinking about this today, how I can't imagine
you spending so much money

on one package of cookies
even though those were his favorites

and he was yours. I thought about
how I lied when you asked

if I'd taken the macaroons when I came
back from school that steamy August day,

how I swore it must have been the nuns
who'd come for coffee. I remember

going to church with you when you
cleaned the sanctuary and how small

you looked in that hospital bed.
Did Dad ever tell you he sneaked me in

to see you because the nurses turned me away?
I remember Dad asking me to walk

with your casket & how I refused,
so sure at seven of what I did and did not want.

Someone told me recently that grief
is love with nowhere to go

which explains why
I still cry when someone says your name.

On Marjorie Drive

She twirls twice mid-living
room & stops. Waits for applause.
Her audience: sisters, two &
daughters, three: me, the oldest,
at her feet.

Holds a pair of my still-tagged,
back-to-school jeans by belt loops,
her thumbs puppet strings.

Those pants—unzipped—
a lopsided jig in her hands.
Her voice, my record-scratch
soundtrack. The refrain always—
always—

> *My pants are smaller than Lisa's*
> *My pants are smaller than Lisa's*
> *Check the tags and see who grew*
> *My size is one number and hers is two!*

I give her what she wants. Giggle
with my aunts & sisters, catch the jeans
she tosses my way.
She pirouettes, bows.

It's Not Like She Didn't Teach Me Anything

Mid-eighties she moved into her father's trailer—
her parole officer agrees it's within
city limits & drug free. I remember

those rooms full of gossiping aunts & wrestling
cousins, the one kitchen counter
crammed with swollen noodles

in weepy gravy & slick, roasted goose.
What never changed: cigarette smoke,
curtain thick.

I wanted to slip through that sliver of light
propel myself on the saggy swing

in Grandpa's otherwise barren backyard.
Back then, my uncle lived in the room
that became my mother's. I'd sneak in,
study the *Hustlers* he stacked thigh deep.

My two little sisters & I visit her
twice a week. Unsupervised visitation

the court says—how do they know it feels
like a funeral since she's come back, like
staring at a long-forgotten relative,

a ghost of her in an open casket?
Hours measured in sitcoms & soap operas. She & I
empty our tips on her faded bedspread.

We work different diners but serve
the same wrinkled, sticky-fingered
men with leery eyes & silent wives.

She's pleased. Her take triples mine.
She draws the Marlboro Red dangling
from her lips. Sucks. Leans in. Snickers.

See, I can still teach you a thing or two.
Bigger tits & tighter tops.

Bragging Rights

I didn't think to write you down.
Now, when I look for clues, I return
to the same old stories:
your Marlboro Reds and Mountain Dew.

You remember this one, don't you, about
when you volunteered as my Girl Scout leader?
Instead of camping you took us to the Holiday Inn.
Sprung for cable and turned the screen to soft-core porn.

You feigned surprise when another girl screamed
from the bathroom, the sight of your spent tampon casually
floating in the bowl too much for her to bear.

You answered all their questions, those girls. Crawled
under a blanket with everyone but me, giggles
and flashlights and your voice, rising above theirs
to shriek: *Lisa's jeans? They're bigger than mine!*

What would I send you for Mother's Day now?

I'd tell you how that night I sneaked away
to the hotel pool, comfy in my sweats and t-shirt, alone
until dawn when the manager found me asleep
with my library book. He thought I'd jumped the fence.

I lied to him until I belonged there & in that instance
I was your daughter. I think you might have been proud
though I don't remember you ever saying.

Before that day I didn't say goodbye,
I remember you saying *At least you have pretty hair.*

In Prison, She

caught the eye of a man she called Jake // said he looked good in his standard issue shoes // said he wrote her notes and passed them during lunch // said she pretended not to blush // said all her girlfriends were jealous // said they took walks around the yard // said he asked what she thought of the gray fuzz of the sun // said he slipped into her cell at lights out // said he brought tape for her cellie's mouth // said she liked the slick of his palm on her lips // said she felt the world open when he offered that line // said her bitch of a roommate liked to watch // said she read her life in the vein of his hand // said rough is not having a cigarette when he left // said we could read his letters when she came home // said pay attention here's where it gets good // said she was in in for the smack // said his slam is smooth as his shiny scalp // said falling makes her spine tingle // said let's invite him for turkey dinner // said you can wear your prettiest dress // said maybe you can call him daddy.

The Sum of Me

Wanted as in *served a purpose*. Add sisters, two. Add Donna Summer, Beach Boys, lobstered skin at the corner pool—all day. *Boys pinch because they like you.* Add babysitting, add sleepovers, add Girl Scouts, add violin. And viola. At 13, ask how she chose my name. *You were supposed to be a Christopher.* Sophomore year, add school newspaper, add debate tournaments, add feathered hair & eye shadow—blue. Add tables to wait, quarters to save. Greedy-fingered men. Add the scholarship, road trip to college. Add hiding behind the campus church, between city traffic and Lake Michigan tide—let the water make the world a conch. Add retail jobs, add a man at Motel 6. I do. Add babies, three. Sign the decree.

It's What I've Got Left

Lacy veil to bone-deep ache

a rosary I choose to not pray

The Sum of Me: Two

Fast forward: kids are grown. I'm alone. I can date now & I do & realize it's not for me—give me the dark of a movie theater, the company of friends. Pages of a book. The moon. Where do I begin now? With long memory but also with deep cabernet, this waterfall in Laos, this yurt in the Mojave Desert.

Self-Portrait as Good Girl

In a studio on the shore forty years
past, I study a photograph
of a man's hands. Fingers
curved around a pocketknife

& his palm a pocket for the thing
he carves—a nub of wood, say,
or a firm, glittered fish. My point:
there's no perspective that makes sense.

The first man I watched hold a knife
taught me new words. Told me
what he does to the wood. His point:
good girls do what they're told. Even now,

that man strobes far corners
of my mind—his fingers calloused
sausage, quick & sure, his yellow
nails, thick & zebraed with dirt. But

his voice. Gritty as a cat's
tongue. He meant every word.

I want to place that man's words
in the worn pocket of the man
behind the glass, the man whose face
I cannot see.

Can I stand at the edge
& watch those words sift
through his soft, safe fingers?
     Watch me.

This Time When We Talk Things Are Different

But you're still right there
in your ratty recliner, Grandma,

bent at the waist to get closer
to me criss-cross-applesauced

at your feet. I have to explain
Payless Shoe Store is no more,

that we can no longer
take these back or

look for a pair that might fit. I study
the mountainous veins

on your hairless legs, trace
spiderwebbed trails from ankle

to knee, finger the hem of your
once-purple dress.

You babble through options, gibberish.
I've already peeled

the shoes, you said, your voice fast,
a piercing boom that rattles

Jesus's sacred heart trapped
on the wall behind

Dollar Store glass. *Peeled*
both pumps like russet potatoes,

you said, left each with a wooden
witch's heel and raw, shiny satin.

They're ready to dye, you whisper
to the air right above

my just-slept hair, your palms extended
as if taking communion.

You said: *It's ok to touch. Please touch.*
Can you help me?

I want these fancy shoes
dishwater gray like the mice

that might stay once the weather
turns mean. I want them to feel like home.

This Wind, Bitter

I.

Kansas wind slipped
through Grandma's window,
seeped through threadbare blankets,
she & I secure.

My toes, blue. Numb
as my fingers when I helped her
at work, elbow-deep
in iced chicken innards.

Oh Hatzya. Give me those toes.
Rosary coiled her palm, dripped from her wrist.
Black beads branded my ankles as she rubbed my feet,
warmed each between her fleshy thighs

II.

In my first Chicago apartment,
the memory of those beads marking
my ankles & her thumbs grooving
the soles of my feet,

she confesses:
*I nod off during Mother Angelica
so I start over & over again,
my Hatzya.*

III.

We buried her on a Friday.
I bought pumps from Payless, gray
to match my mood, the sky,
my too-tight dress.

Kansas winter is soulless. Bitter winds kicked her casket as I shifted foot to foot, toes pinched. Stiff.

A Proper Lady Speaks Not of Regret

Debris.   Coffee can filled with coins

    stashed behind mothballed blankets.

Autumn   first dew, lovely   film reel of ombréd leaves.   Xanthophylls

    carotenoids,   garlands

    rusted gold Sugar Maple and jaundiced Green Ash.

    Candles labeled *Pumpkin Spice* and *Feels Like Home.*

    A credit card   in maiden name.   Unbooked plane

tickets,   itinerary   penned in disappearing ink.

    Golden hour.

Equinox,   settle in   moonshine-spiked cider

    and memory.   Chlorophyll.   Sourwood blaze.

    Blankets of patchwork praise.

Fall,   littered   leaves   from storm drains, drippy.

    Daylight Savings Time,   each room

  with fluorescent glare.   Broken broomstick through

  that front porch   crack, remind the opossum   and her babies

this is not their home.   Mettle.   Grocery money rounded up.   Papers after bedtime   stories,

notes scribbled   standing in line.   Sundown.

         Harvest,   almost-ruined fruit   lava,   cool,

pop—seal.   Gemstoned jars,   friends for coffee. Cookies.

      The friend who says   *the leaves are so much more*   *colorful*

this year.   Winter. What's left   scraped

       from under the steps,   bagged double-knot tight,   toss it

to the curb.   Strangers carry   what remains.   Pocket

          lint.   Molded bread   made toast.   Auxin,

nose-dive,   tumble.   Gone.   This is blue hour.

I Don't Pray Anymore But I Remember the Words

Oh my Jesus,

I learned bead by bead when I was eight,

*Forgive us our sins
save us from the fires of hell*

below, heaven above and me—once married,
limboed, too much a sinner to say
Oh my Jesus,
but pleading, still:

*lead all souls to
heaven*

has conditions. My transgressions, venial, expiation
ingrained bead by bead.
I beg indulgence for having offended you,
Oh my Jesus,
for saying *I do* while thinking *I can't*,
for wasting years yoked,
for lying
with a man I almost loved

Oh my Hatzya,
Grandma's whisper the same, all these years gone,
repeat after me:
Oh my Jesus, forgive me my sins, save

her: this her earnest wish, most fervent plea—
her intentions pure.
Save

> *especially those in most need*
> *of thy mercy.*

But
oh. My Jesus.
She forgets.
The dead cannot pray for themselves.

Grandma, You're 97 Today

Stone flat & slick with sloppy debris splayed
like slapped-on shards of hand-torn paper.
Daisies dyed hot pink and neon green clash
with carnelian leaves plastering the ground.
Nothing here has changed

since you've gone. The wind from the day we buried you
is back. The sky still muddy. You're warm, I hope,
under these layers of dirt and wood. Not in pain,
like those last years,
your body a betrayal.

Do you start the day now with coffee,
rub your father's feet when the sun dips?
I wish I'd met him. Maybe it's enough
you never mentioned him—
but your mother, I remember.

I still have that photo of her, sitting in a tapestry
chair, a scarf covering her head
and knotted under her chin, even indoors.

You were the last to join them here.

Look at that: they've set your party table
with Kudzu & Russian Knapweed, plucked buds
from the beds of relatives here but not invited.
Go have fun. I'll wait right here, busy myself in the dirt,
pull the weeds that litter your plot.

The Quilt You Made for Me Hangs In My Dining Room

It's not one of those prize-winning quilts. You know this,
right? It doesn't look like the perfectly proportioned
tulip rows you planted each year.

Thin rectangles of discard fabrics.
Blue & white polka dots, green & brown plaid.
Orange polyester with fat pink petals & comic book leaves.

Why polyester? Why polka dots?
I remember sitting with you on your bed the day you finished it,
turning it over to see the backing.

All those stitches, Mina, with your locked
fingers, lifetimes of prayers you said while you sewed.
Me, pouty & insistent that you

make it prettier. Me, crying, until you cut a final piece, all the while
telling me it wouldn't fit. A square this time, sky blue base
for a red & white checked heart. I loved that red & white heart.

I sat with you on your bed as you tacked the square to the center
of my baby doll quilt, took it from you when I deemed it done.
I doubt I said *thank you*. I don't remember hugging you

or saying *I love you*. But you know now, right? You know I've carried
this quilt with me from house to house, state to state. That I've kept it
in my babies' cribs, slept with it under my pillow.

Who Loved You, Mina?

I.

I see you kneeling,
fingers deep in fertile ground,

making beds for your tulips.
I'm lying. I never saw you
tend a garden, never watched
you plant a bulb—but I saw flowers

bloom every spring, watched stems whip
with the wind while petals dropped

to the ground, mingled with your
neon green grass.

II.

The funeral announcement I find online says only: daughter, sister, parishioner. Nothing about what candy you ate when no one was looking or the songs you whistled while you scrubbed the sink. Nothing about any movies that left your nose blushed or the books you told others they just had to read.

III.

Nothing about the men you loved.

IV.

To revive
your bones with joy

and surprise—I'd replace
daughter with dancer, sister

with sinner, parishioner
with painter poet paralegal

party pooper paramedic pole dancer—
something with spice.

V.

Your rosary wrapped wrist,

the duty of abstaining
every Friday, you

perched heavy
on the bathtub edge,

scolding me
for the pleasure I felt

when the warm water
rolled down my chest.

VI.

I buy bunches of tulips every spring—scarlet
& fire-licked lemon & wedding dress white.

Teaching Myself at 51

The women who raised me were plain. Devout.
Called whores if they rouged their cheeks
or wore sassy pumps or failed to smile
when poked. They carried babies, mortgages,

their men, precious porcelains.
Little, I watched them garden. Pinched my nose
while they worked manure into the soil, their hands
thick and sticky with stink. I see it now

in the beds they tended—tulips & lilies & daffodils—
bawdy & flamboyant perfect rows kissing their brick homes.
Now I am teaching myself to grow things.
The rosebush I water with manure tea blooms late

every spring, produces one glorious flower, its ruffles
Lady Danger red, its center white wedding dress.
Quiet mornings I plant my knees in the still-wet
ground, watch her solitary stem sway in the Kansas

wind. I like knowing she'll rebloom blind to everything
but her own fire & ice, eagerly alive in the Tickseed
sunrise until her last, shriveled petals slip away, unashamed
by who sees her spent & strewn atop this still-solid ground.

Prolapse: Etymology

An upside-down pear, my doctor says. I tell her it feels more like an orange. Bumpy and ridged, like a too-new rind. *Sometimes I try to push it back to where I imagine it belongs.* Her brow spirals. She nods. Takes notes. Talks about a sling. *Not a big deal.* A hammock to keep that part where God intended. (God. When I was in high school and cramped so bad I couldn't stand, the doctor told my father The Pill would help. Dad objected. Suggested a hysterectomy. *She doesn't want kids anyway.* Besides, if I took The Pill I'd surely have The Sex and God wouldn't like that. Two men, fighting over my uterus while I watched, a mound on that table in a gape-backed gown. Doing nothing is a decision. Every cramp reminded me *God is watching*, reminded me that my corkscrew innards served His greater glory. God's work, the babies that came later, all three glorious with stink, sticky and pure. God's will, their raising. God's plan, their leaving.) Lovely idea, isn't it? I could sleep nude again if that urge hadn't slipped, too, as if in cahoots with the root of me, asking which pieces plan to stay.

Something That Made My Mother Sad

Sad: adj (1) *Affected by unhappiness or grief.*
Mom, I can't imagine how *affected*
you were as a kid
by your alcoholic parents
and twice-broken nose.
Dad told me that your mother,
bourbon-drunk and *unhappy*
to be stuck all day/every day
with the four of you,
found it fun
to goad your father
into disciplining his children.
His hand, her smack.
(I never asked: Did he hit you to shut her up?
Or were they a team, playing tag
with the bridge of your nose?
Did it matter to you, either way?)

(2) *Sorrowful or mournful/expressive of or characterized by sorrow.*
Did your mother ever tuck you in
at night, read a fairy tale?
Or were you like me, rocked to sleep
by fists through walls?
What did you think about
before you fell?
Did you dream
about rhinestone studded boots
or your fingers ringed in gold? Did you ever imagine
your happily ever after? Mysteries
to me, the minutes
that ticked your days.

(3) *Causing sorrow.*
(Notice the verb here.
The agency.)

Sorrow: noun (1) *Distress caused by loss, affliction, disappointment, etc; grief, sadness or regret.*
A mouthful, *sorrow*.
A circle with fangs.

(2) *A misfortune or trouble.*
The schoolgirl you, sassing
back. Still, I bet your teachers
loved you. Just like
the librarians when you slid
your stack of non-fiction
on their desk. Would they have
so openly fawned, said to me,
'how *fortunate* you are,
to have such a smart mom'
if they saw the piles
of Harlequins on your
end table, under the bathroom sinks,
next to your bed?

(3) *The expression of grief, sadness, disappointment, or the like.*
When I was a new mom I couldn't hide
my *disappointment* when I'd walk
into daycare after work only to be
greeted by a screaming child.
The director explained: he isn't *sad*;
he knows he's safe, because you're here.
It's a good thing, his *expression*.
(I found a Polaroid not long
ago. You, me & Uncle Bobby.
Outside, winter. You're wearing
a uniform under your scratchy coat,
a kerchief as a headscarf.
Bobby's holding me but
I'm reaching for you. Beaming,

our smiles so wide
we have no eyes. Was that
safety, then? A blind reach,
a knowing?)

Verb: (1) *To feel sorrow, to grieve.*
What did you *grieve*?
I didn't think to ask until now.
Hindsight. *Regret.*
(Did you *grieve* trading your youth
to be free [to have me] —
or did you *grieve* never being young?)

How I imagine you, now that I'm grown:

feral, *unhappy,* hungry, *distressed,* angry

Mother to mother, will you tell me: what made you *sad?*
If you were to ask me, I'd tell you
what makes me sad is that
the word *unhappy* is defined by what it lacks.

You Turned 69 This April

Astrology.com tells me
you can get along with at least someone.

Your birthstone is the diamond.
Your flower, the sweetpea.

On your birthday the year I was born,
Wikipedia is devoid of an 'on this day' entry.

Ancestry says you were 18 that year.
I always thought younger.

Facebook says I'm right—unless
you lied there, too. I guess

it doesn't matter anymore, does it, Mom?
What matters is that I look for you

in strange places. Bars/bathrooms/kayaking
on the Mekong River/ buying café con leche

in Washington Heights/browsing
the library's romance section.

Why can't truthfinder.com tell me what gnawed
at your core? Does LinkedIn know

what you're proud of? Maybe SocialCatfish
can explain what turned you mean.

Know this: I don't want you back.
I write you as the villain. I cannot stop, cannot.

When Grandma Visits at 4 A.M., She Does So as a Stinkbug

What would you say if I told you I can't help that I scare you now.
The Lord above gave me this crunchy shell. The smell.
Built me to crawl. It's not much different than when
I was there, with you—he's always made damn sure
I knew my place—butchering chickens, ironing shirts
for other women's husbands. Raising my babies.
My babies' babies. Got used to your grandpa leaving
and coming back whenever he damned well pleased.
Leaving again after he got what he wanted.
Remember when I told you the three things
a woman never needs are a husband, a driver's license
and a checking account? Turns out I was right,
but just about one of 'em. But you know that
now. I reckon you also know that creatures like us
only stink when crushed and sweetheart,

I couldn't ask then but I'd really like to know
why did you wait until my wake to use
the pretty words? Strong. Steady. Patient.

Remember how I called you every year on your birthday?
I loved telling you the story, how I went to sleep one person
and woke up as someone new: I was taking a nap
and your daddy sat on the edge of my bed, shook me 'til
I woke up & he said those holy words: Wake up, grandma. She's here.

Oh, my Hatzya, if I still had arms
I'd sprinkle holy water on your blue gray sweater,
whisper with every flick of my wrist
I love you, I love you, oh I love you.

Mina Speaks

No sense in trimming a hangnail—
it will snag again.
Better to use your teeth & pull.
Yes, it will bleed. Not for long
& it stops if you put your finger
in your mouth. Don't make that face
at me—that's our blood. You're worried
about how it looks? Why?
Mary never painted her nails,
did she? You think she stopped
to think about how she looked?
No. She knew she was here
for our Savior. Maybe
someday you'll be a mother.
You're taking notes,
aren't you? I won't be here
to remind you in fifty years
that there's no sense
in tending anything
that's determined to part ways,
no hope in gently caring
for our tender parts:
one way or another,
they'll bleed.

Twitter Says: Be Sure To Write Poems When You're Young

it's a kind of wisdom. Be sure
to keep your hair long as long as you can.
Wear a miniskirt. Wing that glittery green
to a cat's eye. Get the nose ring—but keep it
tasteful. A stud, maybe. Flash your tits
at Mardi Gras before they start to sag. Go wild.
Be sure to travel. Someplace lush. Somewhere
your parents wouldn't dare dream, a place
you need perfume and cute shoes to enjoy—can't
let the locals think you work for a living or that—god
forbid—you're a woman who buys
her own damn dream. Be sure to
save every goddamned detail, write it
in loopy letters with rainbow colored glitter
pens. Not on your phone.
Paper-bound's best for burning.

You, Too, Were a Novena

Those hands of yours—
perpetually in something unpleasant:
a bucket or toilet or someone else's laundry.
Left for the last time
by that husband, with five kids to feed.
You made do. Made, too, bierocks &
strawberry shortcake, spitzbuben & cinnamon rolls.
The butter slick of your hands as they covered mine,
teaching me to roll the dough just tight enough

to keep the sweetness inside. Forty years
of days on that sloppy concrete floor,
reek of grease & blood in the air,
your left hand fisting a pimple-skinned drumstick,
the other a cleaver. Your
wax-fat-coated fingers on mine, thrust into ice,
teaching me—gizzards in the left bucket,
livers in the right. Your chapped, soap-stripped
hands putting the breast of your one allotted meal

on my plate, your face aflame when you damn near sang
Oh no! Hatzya! The wing is my favorite part.
Bless you for teaching me how to properly eat
fries—fat squirts of ketchup & honey. An extra
shake of salt. Bless you for spending 50 cents for four
Pearson mints, for making sandwiches with
pocketed packets of Saltines. Bless you
for the day-off Dillons soup & salad bar
lunches, the hours we talked. Bless you

for the novenas you knelt when I struggled.
The holy water you sprinkled before each goodbye.
Bless you for every $5 bill you stuffed in my pocket
after you retired, each time I came back
home. For a little something—
a snowball or a Dairy Queen. A way, still, to be

in the world when your body kept you glued
to that worn recliner, hands finally idle
but for folding them in prayer, folding those $5 bills

into tiny squares. Bless you in that musty, Section 8
apartment—your first time living alone—trash can
never not full, kitchen dark & empty,
the one window so far across the room.
Bless, too, the Sacred Heart of Jesus—the only décor
on those renter-white walls—& Mother Angelica's voice
tinny from the TV, too often the only voice. Bless you
for grabbing my hand, starting in 8th grade, to say
I might not be here much longer—take something before you go.

Bless you for calling me every birthday
until the summer before you died, telling & retelling our story:
*I went to take a nap—I was so tired, my Hatzya—and then
there was your dad on the edge of the bed, saying 'wake up Grandma.
Grandma, wake up. She's here.'* Bless you for blessing me
with letters when I was two states away, filled
with that handwriting— loopy & sharp—
and that last line, always that last line:
take good care of my Lisa.

She Called Everyone Sweetheart

She baked cookies I wouldn't eat
while she was alive.

"Hertzyen" was the recipe
but she pronounced it *hat-zya*

Hat, not "hurt"
zya, not "zen."

I grew up believing
hat-zya were—that we were—

German & I search now for that recipe
but find "herzjer:"

a German Christmas cookie
that looks like the cookies I remember

but the word—"herzjer"—tangles in my mouth.
I learn that German is not

the same as us: Volga German.
I learn that Volga German is mixed

with Austrian/Bavarian/Russian—
History clutched so tight

stops breathing.
I wish she'd claimed

We are: .
We speak: .

I am: .
I am: .

Lullaby

hat-zya, oh hat-zya, my hat-zya—

For All the People Who Say "But She's Your Mother! There Must Have Been Good Things Too."

Sometimes I think everyone would be happier
if I made things up. I could
talk about that time you took me shopping for a prom dress[1]
or maybe write about how we laced up our shoes
on sweaty summer nights, jogged side by side in the dark.[2]

Oh! I know—I'll write a poem about how I could tell you anything,[3]
how safe I always felt with you.[4] My favorite memory is
how you taught me to keep score at Grandpa's little league games,
the two of us in the dugout with sharpened pencils
and a spiral scoresheet pad. I loved marking a K
for a strikeout, and how you taught me
to make a perfectly reversed K for *struck out looking,*[5] can still feel
your hand on mine tracing the diamond
whenever a player advanced. No wait—maybe
this is the one: how giddy I was
riding shotgun and stopping for snowballs[6] while
we sang along to the radio—the Bee Gees and Crystal Gayle,
Air Supply and ABBA. Maybe that one's happy.
Yes. Let's keep that one happy.

---

[1] But the math is wrong, isn't it? I'd taken you to court to be legally emancipated before I went to prom. We could talk about back-to-school shopping instead, how seamlessly you worked into conversation our vastly different jeans sizes, how your face beamed as you told your coworkers yours were smaller than mine.

[2] I cried from the shin splints, how you wouldn't let me stop because *someone needs to help you work that fat ass off before school starts again.*

[3] You knew I was shoving toilet paper in my underwear when I got my period, didn't you? That I did that for years until we moved in with dad and he bought us pads and tampons?

[4] I mix this memory up: me in the front seat with you, L&L in the back, at the stop sign at 8th & Burgundy on the way into town from your trailer. Is that when you asked if I'd been asked to the dance yet & when I said *no,* you nodded & said, *I always figured you were a dyke—just tell me, I'd rather hear it from you than on the street.* Or was it the time you asked if I'd been asked to the dance yet & when I said *no* you said *didn't think so. No guy wants to fuck a fatty.*

[5] I remember all those times you bragged about the men who hit on you, how you said you knew they couldn't help looking, how you repeated all the words they said.

[6] Until you made me switch to fountain Diet Pepsi, doing me a favor and all, still trying to control my rampantly expanding ass.

I Think of You, Mom, As I Sit In the Driver's Seat of a U-Haul in a Fairfield Inn Parking Lot in Granite City, Illinois, Just This Past March

Two women sit in a blue Nissan, smoking.
Sky streaks behind them like cinema,
my breath ices the air. I watch their hands
teeter-totter to their lips, watch them
drag that smoke with a fervor I wish
I could match. They look old
in that cliched way & their hair
is your same dirty blonde. That Nissan
must smell like our blue Chevelle—the one
with the busted grille we spent hours in,
you chain smoking & me, shotgun,
blissful, ignorant to how smoke settled in my skin,
high on your attention, not knowing
I wouldn't recognize you now, wonder if you're alive.

What Stories Would You Have Told Me If I'd Stayed?

I wish you could have seen my apartment.
Or the reggae bar. Or that weird
performance art I pretended to like.
All that's left is wishing
I'd asked more questions of you
in that battered chair,
TV always humming. I think how lonely
you must have been, stuck there—
how did your mind fill all that time?
Were you angry with with me, how I flitted
in & out, so busy, so busy—a job I barely remember now.

My Therapist Says Joy is the Highest Form of Vulnerability

Grandma made green bean
& dumpling soup, food I make
now when I miss her. My ex said
God that looks nasty. He didn't see
what I did: how she fed five kids
with flour, butter, milk, & a can
of army-green, too-tender, food stamp beans.
How I begged for more. How warm & safe
I felt, her attention all mine.

Maybe someone you loved made chowder. Or stew.
Maybe grilled cheese. It was good, wasn't it—-

COVID Fever Dream of My Estranged Mother

I can't unsee her t-shirt,
still hanging, faded Virgin Mary.
*I would have
given my eyetooth*, she'd said,
for a virtuous daughter.
She smeared her lipstick,
called me a pig.
She sang *don't know when I've been so blue*
while she rinsed our plates.

Yesterday refused to rain.
Her journals stacked, dusty
desperate for color—
I assign hues to match
her moods. Graphite smudges,
a timeline.

Decayed brain
& smoker's lung.
Because our air is poison, she said.
It's a strain,
the doctor said, but of her trachea.
His scrubs are dirty shore blue, she wrote
in the journal she left on the floor
before her lungs turned litter,
before I left her there, waiting.

A Dependent Clause

when all God's children ask: *would you still love me*

—if

Grandma, I Didn't Get to Tell You

I didn't know my kid would be queer or
they'd sunray a room, throw colors as techno
as the Lite Brite Curtis & I poked in fourth grade
before he died. I miss him. Why didn't we talk
about that?

When he died I asked mom to drive me to school.

Let's pretend, even though the priests profess otherwise,
that my kid is a beautiful, beloved child. Like Curtis.
Let's pretend that being queer, like having leukemia, isn't a choice.
Do I have your attention now?

Spite me. That's right—get good & mad.
Blessed are the persecuted, for theirs
is the kingdom of God.

Dear Third Born Child, I Promise I'm Trying. Love, Mom.

The felled oak looks like a one-eyed bird, its freakish beak ready to swallow its beloved trunk, rooted so deep it cannot fall even though it's been split in thirds. I tell you its branches are gnarled like my Aunt Hilda's hands, how she wrapped her knotty fingers around her cane, switched it back and forth to swat the air when she was sour or sad. My father, your grandpa, answers *God can fix all broken things and Hilda, she was broken but not like this, this here is trash—see the rot, it's run straight through.* I think he's talking about you because he motions your way, waves his hand like it's a magic wand strong enough to take your gay away. If you hear him, if he upsets you, you hide it well with a pivot, a pose, a flip of your favorite feathered boa around your otherwise naked neck. When he says broken he means not going to church, means saying their instead of her, means boys not liking girls and the other way around, means different, your kind of different the worst kind. But God can fix all broken things and because my father is a good Christian he's here to do God's work. Like when he forced my left-handed sister to eat with her right, howled until her delicate fingers choked the spoon, sent her to school with oatmeal trails from collar to crotch because there's right and not right and we owe God the glory and penance for our sins. A black cat climbs the wrecked V at the tree's snapping point, offers the tree its paw like a newborn reaching for their mother. You watch me watch my father watch this cat and I remember what a proud papa my dad was, how he cooed when you were tiny, blew raspberries on your Buddha belly. I recall his voice as he whispered *well aren't you perfect,* can still hear the susurrus of your curled fist on his stubbled chin. Now your fists whip the air as you twirl from one mucky leaf to another, hopscotching your way through this wreckage. I close my eyes and offer thanks for your contagious joy, for his warm hand on my shoulder. He leans in, the whiskey of his voice a swarm of bees I cannot swat away; *it's not the child I blame—something in you must have made her this way. Or else she's being punished for your sins.*

Notes for My Daughter as She Plans Her Most Public Assault[1]

Carefully choose a plausible aggressor, even better if he's had a brush or two with law enforcement. Avoid frat boys, legacy boys, football gods, swim team stars. Daddy's buddies and money and all. Be sure to put your best foot forward: pick the right clothes,[2] the perfect color lipstick.[3] Remember to smile.

Choose your company for the night wisely: three is a good number, but only if all three will testify so it's best to plan for backups. You never know who might fall ill, who might refuse to remember, who might need to repay a debt. Make sure at least one has the stomach to watch it all go down—talk to this friend first, assure her she's being your best friend when she doesn't turn away, when she memorizes the curling corner of your attacker's lip, notices the brand name of his shoes. Make watching easy for this friend; for this to happen, you have to lead your rapist to an open space, a place easily accessed by others. Steer clear of basements, abandoned buildings, his backseat in a quiet park. Make sure you ask a different friend for a ride home. Work on your talking points now: if this friend doesn't mention your torn clothing, your smeared lipstick, find a way to casually bring it up in conversation. Remember to take a selfie with this friend—don't forget to smile. Better yet, video the ride.[4] Geo tag it. Back it up to the cloud.

Practice giving your testimony. Stand before the mirror, repeat every detail until you can do so dry eyed. Watch your mannerisms: do you tuck your hair behind your ear? Maintain eye contact too long? Shift from side to side? Stop it. Practice saying I'm sorry and of course and yes, sir. Remember this isn't an admission of wrongdoing. It's expected so please understand: if you fail to recount the event just right, the jury of your peer's attackers will dismiss you without hearing another word you say.

---

[1] I want nothing more than for you to never need this. Statistics say you will, that I did, that two of the three friends you met at freshman orientation already have. When this time comes you'll be forced to learn a new language. You'll learn to scan bloated briefs for hidden clues, to read between the lines.

[2] Nothing too short, too tight, too sheer, too skimpy, too pretty, too complementary, too revealing, too kinky*, too interesting, too provocative, too feminine, too, too, too. *Nothing that might stoke a clichéd fantasy: librarian, cheerleader, teacher, nurse, secretary, nun. Yes, nun.

[3] This is important: it's not about the best color to complement your skin; it's about the best color that shows up on photos. No nudes, no beige, no fleshtone lipsticks. No. You need MAC Lady Danger or Dior 999. No glosses; they rub off too easily. You need a good, old-fashioned, matte stain. You need it to leave a mark.

[4] You'll need enough storage on your phone to capture video, so I've prepaid for unlimited cloud storage in perpetuity. The good folks at Apple offer a mother/daughter plan.

Do you remember what it means to be conciliatory?[5] Choose your wardrobe for the inquisition: tasteful, professional, but not marmish; you want to strike that delicate balance between Jackie and Marilyn, Hepburn and Bardot. Solid colors look best on camera. Keep your hair on the long side but be sure it's shiny and neat; the men asking the questions tend to prefer it that way. A little makeup but not too much.[6] Glasses might help you look smarter. Wear a watch—don't ask me why, but I read somewhere that leaders and people of worth wear watches. Think back to when we played dress-up and sat at your tiny table for cups of invisible tea: remember how we practiced perfect posture, posed our pinkies in the most lady-like way? This is dress-up too, a grown-up kind of pretend.

After the assault: carefully undress and package your clothing in gallon-sized Ziploc bags. Swab under your nails, inside your mouth, wherever your rapist penetrated you. Save the cotton swabs, mark each by body part. Label everything appropriately and store it all in our safety deposit box.[7]

Now it's time to make your phone calls: representative's office, press 2 to report details of your most recent attack; doctor's office, press 3 to leave a message; police department, press 1 to be directed to the automated assault clearing line; each friend with you the night of the attack, to remind them they witnessed your undoing. Take notes in your calendar, including the time of each call.[8]

A note about calling your representative's office: lines start to jam mid-day so make yourself a cup of tea and dial before it's cool enough to chug. Have regional office numbers ready; you might have to call multiple lines before you find someone willing to help. When a staffer answers, ignore the routine of it all, the robotic tone with which your report is accepted. But don't be fooled. Be ready for the hoops, for hold time. They want to see if you can hack it, if you have what it takes to persist. You do. Steep more tea. Stand at your open window and watch a squirrel scramble along your deck rail, flatten itself when it notices you. Watch leaves change from green to grunge

---

[5] Conciliatory (adj): intended or likely to placate or pacify. Appeasing. Pleasing. Say yes ma'am and no sir, please and thank you. Avert your eyes so as not to appear aggressive. Use your sweetest, quietest voice. Nuance here matters, so I need you to practice: it's acceptable for your voice to crack, for you to seem as if you're about to cry but not to show too much emotion, to cry too much, to break down. See: histrionics, hysterical, unreliable witness.

[6] This would be a good time to wear the nude, the beige, the flesh-tone gloss. Clinique Long Last Glosswear in Tender Heart or Bobbi Brown High Shimmer Lip Gloss in Bare Sparkle are nice.

[7] I've included your name on our family box; when you visit, you'll see my calendars and those that belong to your grandmother, your aunt, my best friend from 2nd grade. It's our shared time capsule, an addendum to your baby book, your yearbooks, your stacks of posed photos and saved greeting cards.

[8] It seems a bit too much, I realize, but even our First Lady says women need "really hard evidence" to even suggest an assault occurred.

to rust, but don't relent to the romantic notion of a gorgeous Fall; instead stand witness to the dying of it all. You're strong enough to see the difference.

Keep your checklist handy. It's your job to make sure the staffer records your assaulter's name and social security number, the exact time and coordinates of the assault, and names of your corroborating witnesses. Once you've heard this staffer read the information back to you, ask for a confirmation number. Write it in your calendar in the square marked today. Store that calendar in a Ziploc bag, in our family box (there are extra checklists there; grab one before you go so you're ready for the next time).

Call me. Anytime. Day, night, drunk, sober, happy, sad, worried, mad. Once, twice, thirty-seven times. Just call.

Remember: this list of instructions applies only to planned attacks. There will be others—many will be micro and seemingly meaningless: a man might cup your buttocks at a crowded concert and feign ignorance when you make eye contact; another might follow you down the street, leer, offer assessments of your body; yet another might pose as your boss, your teacher, your preacher, a relative and whisper in your ear, suggest you never tell. Some will cut emotional scars; others will leave bruises. All will hurt. I have no instructions for these save my own stories and the stories of women I love. Is this my greatest failing, as your mother, how I send you into the world with a shield so easily ripped apart?

One final note: treat yourself kindly. Work time into your daily schedule to reflect. Bullet-point details of your day, every day, in your calendar. I read once about a husband who, before he died, arranged for a flower delivery to his wife on every subsequent birthday. He left dozens of notes with his florist, dates of future deliveries penned in curly-cue cursive on heavy, cream envelopes. The idea of flowers makes me smile, but only until I remember that flowers, too, die and it's up to us (the mothers, the daughters) to throw them away, mop up the mess. I can't bear the thought of burdening you with that, sweet soul; I can't send you a monthly reminder of shriveling. Of rot. Not when it's already in and around us, not when we are expected to swallow it all. Instead of flowers I've arranged a delivery of pens, a new bunch every birthday. Forgive me for spoiling the surprise but I can't wait for whatever comes next; I'm too happy remembering how your face lit up on your eighth birthday when you unwrapped a Costco-size box of gel pens: rainbow rows of every color that you used for homework, for sketching, for endearing notes you left on my pillow on random afternoons, your penmanship awkward and loopy and tirelessly joyful. My one wish: don't save these pens for a special day. Use every pen so often the ink runs dry: grassy green for grocery lists, ocean-water blue to send cards to your brothers, tattoo black to write poetry, essays, letters to your elected officials. On assault days, use one of the red pens—not the red of Valentine's Day hearts or summer watermelon slurp. Write the details you know others will want to hear in cherry juice red, blotchy and real.

Protecting the Nest

On a random Tuesday, dad says:

Oh, my mother. My mother. You know everyone thought she was so sweet. Wouldn't hurt a fly. But there were snakes under the porch & the landlord didn't care so here she came, in her apron, carrying a pot of boiling water. I watched her pour water through the missing slat, watched her kill those snakes.

Watched her do what no man would.

Mary, Do You See My Child
In All Their Heavenly Splendor?

Tell me what you saw
that gloriously sun-soaked day:

did you see the splintered stained-glass reverie—
rainbows cast across each pew—

or did you see my pride
as I watched my youngest child

walk down the aisle, white satin dressed,
pink rosebuds in their hair?

Did you marvel with me, Mary,
at how small the communicants seemed,

eyes fixed on the floor, fingers tulipped
in prescribed prayer, chanting words I know by heart:

body & blood of Christ. Consubstantial with
the Father, through Him all good things are made.

I taught them to recite those words, too.
Called them what my father & the church

named them: Girl. Catholic.

Until my baby confessed, told me
they're more bowtie than dress,

but neither, exactly.
& it was then I began to see.

The Church's mysteries: sorrowful, dolorous
but my child's eyes: joyful, glorious.

To thee I do come, Mary, before thee I stand, sinful
my shame sour as lilies left after a celebration.

I implore they help: despise not my petitions,
but in thy mercy hear and answer me.

Mary, I offer penance only to my child,
alms for every moment they felt othered.

And you, fellow mother, O mother
of the Word Incarnate, you, in that chair

to the right of your son, your words a whisper
in his ear: for you I leave these tulips, wilted, at your feet.

Still) Want/ed To

Skip the line.   Pierce my nose.   Ink my clavicle.

Speak my mind.   Go commando.   Dance on a pole in the nude

with the lights on.

Play the violin & the cello & the piano & the sax.

Beg for forgiveness. Repent. Relent. Give up regret for Lent.

Build a bonfire.   Leave zucchini on a neighbor's porch.   Chat

over a backyard fence.   Invite folks for dinner.   Be the last
to leave.   Be comfortable in   silence.   Be

there when she died.   See him,   her,   all of them   again.

Never get pregnant//have kids//live together//say I do//yoke myself//
give myself//lose myself to another//in another.

Never say never.

Ask her why. Ask her why. Ask her why. Ask her why. Ask her why.
Ask her why.   Ask her.

Fly to Italy/Greece/Spain/Thailand/Switzerland/Iceland/Portland.

Stay
        in Chicago.   Stand alone
in the ocean.   Let the waves have their way.   Ride
the waterfall.   Camp.   Turn starlight to cinema,

crickets to concert.   Ride in a limo.   Make

reservations.   Know which fork to use.   Smudge

      a seductive cat eye.   Rock a red lip.   Master

Manolos   but only in bed &   only when I feel like it.

Perfect Pigeon pose   & the handstand   —   with lotus legs.

     Perfectly garnish   an Old Fashioned.   Eat lobster

fresh   from the ocean   floor.   Shrimp & scallops, too.

        Run a 5k.   Run.

Blue Mist

I stole makeup from my mother
in sixth grade—circled my eyes Blue Mist,
lined & mascaraed them knock-out black.
It took weeks for her to notice, me
in the backseat
inquisitor in the rear-view.
My hair was shiny copper & flipped
like Farrah Fawcett & my mother
couldn't tell me a goddamned thing—
not that the blue was garish, not that
the mascara was sloppy & narrowed
my eyes. How could she,
too-young herself? Now I know:
To highlight the hazel of my eyes
I need soft shades of camel and butterscotch.
Pure Plum liner to flirt
with the flecks of green I've only recently seen.
In another life I'd call her. We'd laugh.
Maybe she'd tell her grandkids: *that blue eyeshadow—*
Lord, you should have seen her!

Smirk

Blame my mother's body, her slick
lying tongue—every word

a jab, sport she learned from her
mother, bourbon-drunk & mean.

Blame my mother's cold discontent.
From her I learned to clock a man's

gaze, to rate women's bodies 1-10.
Blame my mother's body, her quick

& perfect smirk. She blamed
her mother, her father, my father—

how can I blame my mother's body,
that open, reliable bruise? So what

if I was her ticket out? So what
if she asked for the shot

to dry her milk, if she
pawned us off on anyone willing?

So what if she became her mother
not bourbon-drunk but mean?

And look at me: mean as I want to be,
blaming my mother's body,

my every word a jab.

Alternate Reality in Which I Return Home After Caring for My Mother

The last slurred *lift another to my lips.* Dark house riding.
I swaddle the antennaed TV in her favorite blanket,
       lonely.
I am drained, one fork alone in our sink,
her shoes still bagged, dropped on the table.

NOTES

The word *hatzya*, which appears throughout, is a Volga German derivation of the German word *herzjen*, which is both the name of a cookie we made at Christmas and used by my Grandmother to mean *sweetheart*. It's spelled phonetically, as she spelled it.

Reference is made to Mother Angelica, who was a Roman Catholic nun with a television show called "Mother Angelica Live."

The poem *I Don't Pray Anymore But I Remember the Words* includes the Fatima Prayer.

The poem *Mary, Do You See My Child In All Their Heavenly Splendor* includes part of the Memorare Prayer.

ACKNOWLEDGMENTS

"Dear Reader" is after Randall Horton's "Dear Reader"

The phrase "trauma and long memory" in "The Sum of Me" is borrowed from "Rain On a September Morning" by Valerie A. Smith

"Something That Made My Mother Sad" was inspired by a prompt from a friend that said "Something that made your mom sad" and is after A. Van Jordan's *From*

"Twitter Says: Be Sure To Write Poems When You're Young" was inspired by a tweet, the origin of which I did not document and do not remember. I apologize to the original creator for this lack of attribution.

"(Still) Want/ed To" is after Sharon Dolin's "Should Have"

"Smirk" is after Marie Howe's "My Mother's Body"

Thanks to the following journals for publishing these poems, in earlier versions:

Anti-Heroin Chic "Bragging Rights"

Bacopa Literary Review "Dear Third Born Child, I Promise I'm Trying"

Bear Review "Party Line" (nominated for the Pushcart Prize)

Cagibi "My Great Aunt Tells Me I Am Such a Good Girl"

December Magazine "In the Down of the House of the Man on the Stoop" and "In Prison, She"

Hole In the Head Review "Self-Portrait as Good Girl," "Something That Made My Mother Sad"

Lily Poetry Review "Notes for My Daughter As She Plans Her Most Public Assault"

MER "She Called Everyone Sweetheart"

The Normal School "Teaching Myself at 51" under the title "And Now that I'm 51."

Pinch Journal "Still Life With Recipe Card"

River & South Review "When Grandma Visits at 4 A.M., She Does So as a Stinkbug"

South 85 Review "Prolapse: Etymology" (2022 finalist for *The Best of the Net Anthology*)

GRATITUDE

Eileen Cleary, thank you for believing in my work, seeing past my shortcomings and helping me create a book I'm proud of. It's a marvel to watch you work and a privilege to learn from you.

Meg Kearney, thank you for creating an MFA program that welcomed me and helped me fall in love with the work of so many others. Randall Horton, Dzvinia Orlowsky, Anne-Marie Oomen, and Laure-Anne Bosselar, you were the perfect mix of poetry mentors. Thank you. Iain Haley Pollack, Nicole Terez Dutton, Kathleen Aguero, José Angel Araguz, Amy Hoffman, Steven Huff, Laura Williams McCaffrey, Josh Neufeld, David Yoo, Sandra Scofield, & Renee Watson, thank you for teaching me how to write by sharing your own remarkable work. Elizabeth Mercurio, Quintin Collins, Daniel Summerhill, Eileen Cleary, Rebecca Kirk Connors, Lisa Charnock, Ellen Austin-Li, Elizabeth Adilman, Claire McCabe, & Rhonda McDonnell, you were the best poetry cohorts I could wish for. Ann Breidenbach, thank you for introducing me to this community & Beth Richards, I'm so glad you're part of my Solstice family.

Rebecca Kirk Connors, Lisa Charnock, & Trish Bogle, this book would not exist without you. Thank you for sharing this love of poetry, for patiently reading revision after revision, and for your countless insights and edits.

Trish & Chuck Bogle, thank you for literally providing shelter in the storm, for loving and nurturing poetry (and poets) in your myriad ways and (not at all least) for all the fun confetti!

Becca, you are a brilliant and steadfast partner. I love what we're building with The Notebooks Collective.

Eric Boermeester, Garvan Giltinan, & Monika Kalina, workshopping not-poetry with you is a blast and I am a better writer for it.

Andy Smart, you convinced me I could write a poem. Thank you.

Marcia Hurlow, Maril Crabtree, & Annie Newcomer, thank you for welcoming me into your fold.

Mark, I write most and best when traveling & because of you I travel. Thank you for getting me out of the house, even if it is just to hang out at yours.

Bet, Cheryl, Katherine, Sarah, and Zach, thank you for asking about my writing, celebrating with me when I had good news & encouraging me when I didn't. How lucky am I to call you friends.

This list will never be complete and there are countless more names that belong here, for countless reasons. To all of you, my unending gratitude and appreciation.

About the Author

Lisa Allen's (she/her) work can be found in *Lily Poetry Review, December Magazine, Anti-Heroin Chic, Bear Review* and *MER,* among others. She has received numerous Pushcart Prize and Best of the Net nominations and was a 2022 Best of the Net finalist for her poem "Prolapse: Etymology," published by *South 85 Journal.* Lisa holds an MFA in Creative Nonfiction and an MFA in Poetry, both from the Solstice Low Residency MFA in Creative Writing Program at Lasell University, where she was a Michael Steinberg fellow. With Poet Rebecca Connors, she co-founded and co-directs the online creative space The Notebooks Collective (TheNotebooksCollective.com).

www.ingramcontent.com/pod-product-compliance
Lightning Source LLC
LaVergne TN
LVHW090036080526
838202LV00046B/3842